G000075295

The Dar...... Mountain Bike Guide — Peter Barnes

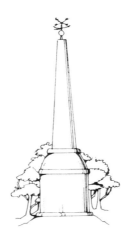

OBELISK PUBLICATIONS

PLATE ACKNOWLEDGEMENTS
Front cover by Susan Barnes, back cover by Peter Barnes
All other photographs Chips Barber
Maps ι drawn from an out-of-copyright source by Sally Barber

First published in 1994, Reprinted in 1995 and 1996 by
Obelisk Publications, 2 Church Hill, Pinhoe, Exeter, Devon
Designed by Chips and Sally Barber
Typeset by Sally Barber
Printed in Great Britain by
The Devonshire Press Limited, Torquay, Devon

The Dartmoor Mountain Bike Guide

INTRODUCTION

Dartmoor is often regarded as 'The Last Great Wilderness' in Southern England. In reality half of its 365 square miles is farmed and/or cultivated and much of the remainder owes its wild nature to the activities of man going back nearly six thousand years.

The moors existed long before the designation of Dartmoor as a National Park in 1951. Remains on the moor going back as far as the Neolithic age (or 4000 BC) make this area one of the most important archeological sites in Europe. Following the Neolithic and Bronze ages the miners of tin, arsenic and silver left their mark as did the great open cast pits of the China Clay industry and a century of military activity over much of the high moors. The inhospitable nature and granite foundations of Dartmoor mean that it remains, however, an area of bleakness, legend and romance, an area where if you are lucky you are just as likely to meet a fox or even, if you are very lucky, an otter as other people.

It is now the force of recreation that is the biggest threat to the moors and along with pony trekking, mountain biking has the potential to be one of the worst culprits. Remember that a peat bog, which has taken hundreds of years to develop, can be churned up in moments by the reckless action of a few riders.

It will be obvious to anyone who knows the moors that this guide contains no routes over the high moors. This is not to say that there are no rights of way over the wilder parts of Dartmoor – there are. The Dartmoor National Park Authority has however, expressed concern that these routes are highly environmentally sensitive. It is in keeping with the ecological awareness and aims of this guide, therefore, that these routes are excluded. If you want to cycle these routes, and they include some of the legendary crossing routes of the moor, it is worthwhile bearing in mind that they are on the high moor with all that entails in the way of navigation and remoteness.

WHEN TO RIDE

The West Country enjoys some of the best all year round weather in the UK, it also has some of the wettest! Cycling in the winter has some major advantages, not least the chance that you will have the route to yourself and if you pick your day well there is a good chance of fine weather. The down side is that the ground will be wet, this is particularly relevant on the moors, and not only will the going be harder but you may do more environmental damage. It is also worth bearing in mind that the West Country 'shuts' for the winter, many shops and cafes may be closed and pubs often revert to limited opening hours; accommodation is easier though.

In the summer everything will be open, so the essential ice cream stops can be guaranteed! There will however, also be a lot more people around, narrow roads and car parks in popular areas can become very congested as can favourite cycle routes. The major plus is that moors partially dry out, even more so in recent years, so that you can enjoy riding on firm ground without leaving tyre tracks behind. If you particularly want to see the archaeological remains of the West Country, bear in mind that many of the smaller stone rows and hut circles can be hidden by tall bracken at this time of year. It is also surprising how long the daylight hours are in the middle of the year and this might be something you want to take advantage of by doing evening rides.

ACCESS

There is still a large amount of confusion over what constitutes a **Public Right of Way**. In simple terms they are:

PUBLIC ROADS — don't be put off by the term road, there are a large number of UNCLASSIFIED COUNTY ROADS which are no longer in a condition to be used by vehicles but make good cycle routes. They are not, however, distinguished from ordinary roads (or private roads/drives) on the OS maps.

PUBLIC FOOTPATHS —are usually well marked on OS maps and are distinguished on the ground and signs by yellow arrows/discs. Cyclists have NO right of way on a Public Footpath.

BRIDLEWAYS — are open to walkers, horses and cyclists, in practise they are the main routes for off-road cycling. Remember that cyclists are required to give way to horses and walkers. As well as being marked on OS maps they are distinguished by blue arrows/discs on signs and markers.

GREEN LANES — are an historical feature of the English countryside and are usually unsurfaced, hedged tracks. The term has no legal meaning and unless the track falls into one of the above categories, there is no right of way.

RUPP — or Road Used as a Public Path is another old expression although one that is still used. They tend to have at least Bridleway status. At present RUPPs are being reclassified as one of the above.

CYCLE PATHS — are dedicated routes, usually of bridlepath status. There is only one cycle path in this guide, which is dealt with in Route One.

DARTMOOR COMMON LAND — The Dartmoor Commons Act of 1985 gave a wide range of rights and access over land that has been designated as Common Land.

There is, however, no right to cycle on any open land, and that includes the Commons.

MILITARY ROADS — There is a considerable road network extending south from Okehampton into the heart of the Northern Moor. Most of these roads are impassable by normal traffic and can make a fun day out. However, bear in mind the following: right of way is historical rather than legal, it is not guaranteed; don't be tempted to ride off the roads, the open moor has no right of way over it; the roads extend into the firing ranges, see details on page 6.

DISUSED TRAIN LINES — Incredible as it may seem there is no automatic right of way over most of the disused train lines which cross parts of the south moor. Although some of these ex-lines are now extremely popular cycle routes the right of way is often off to one side on the open moor, if at all. The National Park Authority is attempting to negotiate rights of way on some of the more popular of these lines.

NOTE — on the open moors in particular, the right of way is often indistinguishable and is identified merely by an arbitrary line on the map. Do not use this as an excuse to ride off the trail. Mountain Bike access is a contentious issue in many parts of the West Country and it is up to all of us to try and improve its image.

In many parts of the West Country there are highly sensitive areas, both environmentally and/or historically. Please – do not cycle through any archaeological sites and avoid any areas, such as peat bogs where you are going to leave an indelible reminder of your passage. Some of the routes in this guide do use bridlepaths on the open moor, so if in doubt – WALK.

The Dartmoor National Park Authority publish a leaflet explaining the rights of cyclists in the park. They are also intending to publish a map showing what they consider to be the most suitable rights of way within the National Park. The Dartmoor Tourism Initiative publish a leaflet about the Plym Valley cycle path.

WARNING — THE LAW

The Devon and Cornwall Police do not intend turning a blind eye to bikes being carried on racks on the back of cars. For this to be legal there needs to be lights and number plate clearly visible, this will usually entail buying a light board to hang on the back of the rack. Be warned that this is a fineable offence and the police will be treating it as such.

SAFETY AND EQUIPMENT

It would be a mistake thinking that because you are cycling rather than walking you can ignore the basic rules of mountain safety. Although there are no 'mountainous' regions in the South West, Dartmoor, Bodmin Moor and some of the upland areas can all seem pretty remote if you get into trouble. Likewise the weather throughout the West Country, and Dartmoor in particular, can change violently and even locals are regularly caught out by unexpected mist or storms.

If you are not a mountaineer already there is some very good background reading available. Eric Langmuir's book *Mountaincraft and Leadership* is excellent although rather heavy going. The British Mountaineering Council do a very good condensed version in booklet form called *Safety on Mountains*.

WEATHER FORECASTS

The national forecasts tend not to be so useful in the very localised conditions which prevail in the West Country. There are a number of local forecast services available which are more reliable. The best places to find the relevant details for your area are the local outdoor sports shops. The phone number for the local weatherline service is 0891 500404.

FIRST AID

It is probably fair to say that a cyclist is more likely to get injured than a walker. The best way of learning first aid is to go on a course run by either The British Red Cross or The St John Ambulance. Even if it only gives you greater peace of mind it is never time wasted.

Likewise you should always carry a simple first aid kit. Remember, however, that first aid done badly can often be worse than no first aid at all!

In the event of an emergency remember the following: remove the casualty, and the group, from any source of danger.

Injuries are rarely fatal, cold and shock are: keep the casualty warm, sheltered and reassured.

Treat any injuries in the following order: breathing, bleeding, breaks, burns. It is usually a mistake to give the casualty food and drink.

SEND FOR HELP

— the Dartmoor Rescue Group is called out via the police (999)
— they will need the following information:
    – location of casualty, grid reference and description
    – nature of the injury
    – number of casualties (if more than one!)
    – size, age and experience of group
    – the phone number you are calling from (stay by the phone)

GROUP SIZE

Although it can be a wonderful experience, try not to ride alone, especially in the wilder moorland areas – it only takes one tree root to land you on your head! Three or four is a good group size to work to, any more and you are becoming an intrusion on the landscape.

It is always a good idea to carry some form of personal identification and also to let someone know where you are going and when you intend to return.

FIRING RANGES

There are a number of ranges on the moor, indeed the majority of the north moor is covered by live ranges, although none of the routes in this guide go into the range areas. The range boundaries are marked by red and white poles. When there is firing taking place red flags are flown by day, with red lights replacing them at night. Details of when the ranges are in use can be found in Post Offices, Police Stations, Libraries, National Park Information Offices and Friday's 'Western Morning News'.

CLOTHING

It is not compulsory to spend huge amounts of money on the latest dayglow lycra in order to go out onto the hills on a bike. It is, however, a good idea to spend enough to ensure that your day out isn't ruined by being wet, cold and miserable all day. Wearing layers of clothing is the ideal solution as not only is it more effective at trapping warm air, but it also allows you to peel layers off, and on, to regulate your temperature. It is a mistake not to take waterproofs and spare jumpers with you when you go onto the moors. A windproof is always a sensible thing to cycle in as often a waterproof is far too hot.

Don't forget a helmet, they're even trendy to be seen in now – there is no excuse not to wear one. Note the ANZI and SNELL Institute safety standards.

MAPS AND OTHER ITEMS

It is always a good idea to use the 1:25 000 Outdoor Leisure Series map if one is available with the 1:25 000 Pathfinder Series as a (rather expensive) second choice. The 1:50 000 Landranger Series are, however, excellent in their own right, although they lack the detail of the larger scale 1:25 000 maps. The 1:25 000 Outdoor Leisure Series map for Dartmoor is an excellent, up to date, map. Its only drawback is it is about the size of a bedsheet (or at least it feels like it when you are trying to fold it in the wind!)

It is worth investing in some sort of case to keep your map dry unless you buy one of the laminated versions now available. Also a compass – the 'Silva' type is the easiest to use. As with the map, it is no good carrying it if you can't use it.

Plenty of food and drink can never be a mistake, the amount of energy and liquid that can be used up whilst cycling is incredible. Think about investing in a steel flask for colder days.

A whistle is a good way of attracting attention in a crisis. The international distress signal is six long blasts followed by a minute's break and then repeated.

Other gear worth taking is a survival bag, of the big plastic variety, which can be bought cheaply from camping shops and could just be worth every penny.

YOUR BIKE

The make of bike that you use is largely irrelevant providing it is up to the job. Some of the routes in this guide can be done on a touring bike providing care is taken. There is certainly no need to spend hundreds of pounds on the latest state of the art machine in order to complete any route in this guide. The most important part of the bike/rider combination is the knowledge and expertise of the rider.

The quickest way to ruin your bike is to ride like a maniac, be aware of your limitations and the limitations of your bike.

Bear in mind the following:

Lights – not having lights on your bike is now an on-the-spot fine offence in much the same way as many motoring offences. Likewise with a rear reflector, which is likely to be more effective than a light half the time anyway.

Drinking and riding – some of the routes in this guide include mentions of pub stops – please don't forget that drinking and riding is little different from drinking and driving, not least in the eyes of the law.

Washing your bike – is not only the best way to extend the life of your bike it is also the time when you are likely to spot a problem before it becomes serious.

Don't forget to lubricate any parts that need it after washing if you don't want your bike to become a mass of rust.

Tools and spares – at some stage your bike is going to let you down and you are going to need some form of tool kit and spares. There is, in general, a lot of nonsense talked about tool kits and people seem to swing from not carrying anything to carrying far too much. In essence for each bolt, nut or screw on your bike you need something that will undo it and/or tighten it. Usually this boils down to a couple of Allen keys, a small adjustable, or bike, spanner, a couple of screwdrivers and a pair of pliers.

I see little point in carrying such things as spare spokes and cone spanners on day trips – are you really going to sit down and start doing this type of repair on the open moors? The emphasis should be on bike first aid – do enough to get home.

As for spares, the obvious, and most important, one to carry is a spare inner tube, valve, pump and tyre levers. I tend to carry a couple of spare tubes and leave the puncture repair kit at home. The day I get three punctures I'm giving up! It is also a good idea to carry some assorted spare cables for brakes and gears. Remember, however, that replacing some cables is a tedious job and it might be worthwhile to stick to the first aid principle.

If you are in a group of riders avoid doubling up on tool kits, but make sure that the tools available do fit all the bikes in the group. It is always sensible if everyone carries their own inner tubes, levers and pump – it is always the person who forgets that gets the puncture!

CYCLE TRAILS IN DEVON AND CORNWALL

Unlike some parts of the country there are only a small number of cycle trails in the West Country, they are:

Devon

Plym Valley Cycle Path – this 8 mile long Cyclebag organised path is included in Route one. It starts just outside Plympton and at present ends pretty much in the middle of nowhere. There are plans to extend it but at the moment nothing solid is in the pipeline.

Totnes to Buckfastleigh – this is a Sustrans route, which is only just beginning; much of the route is still under negotiation.

Bellever Forest – is a 3 mile route set up by the Forestry Commission on tracks in their plantation near Postbridge on Dartmoor.

The Tarka Trail – is actually a long, 120 mile, walking route in north Devon. Around twenty miles of it is rideable along the old Southern Railway Line as it runs from Barnstaple to Bideford and then follows the River Torridge upstream.

West Devon (Sticklepath) Cycle Route – is a 30 mile circular route starting, and finishing, at Sticklepath on the northern edge of Dartmoor. The route, by West Devon Borough Council and others, is not a trail as such as it actually follows minor country lanes, not a dedicated cycle path.

West Devon (Tavistock) Cycle Route – is again a West Devon Borough Council project. This route offers 26 or 11 mile options through the lanes of West Devon, starting from Tavistock.

Leaflets describing all of the above routes can be found in Tourist Information Centres in Devon. The larger offices run by the Dartmoor National Park Authority are particularly helpful.

CORNWALL

The Camel Trail – is a popular, and sometimes very crowded, 15 mile long trail which follows the old Southern Railway Line, much of it alongside the River Camel. This trail, which is managed by the Camel Valley Project, runs from Bodmin to Padstow on the coast. The section between Wadebridge and Padstow, along the estuary of the Camel, is very popular.

Cardinham Woods – is a Forestry Commission Plantation near Bodmin. It contains a number of signposted walking routes and a cycle trail of approximately 5 miles.

Leaflets describing these routes can be found in Cornish Tourist Information Centres.

OFF ROAD IN OTHER AREAS

It will come as a surprise to many people that Devon and Cornwall are not wonderful for off road cycling.

The first, and very important, point to make is that the COAST PATH is not a bridlepath and almost nowhere on the path is there any right of way for cyclists. Indeed cycling is causing erosion problems on parts of the path. This is particularly true at Padstow where cyclists come up from the Camel Trail.

Cornwall – Bodmin Moor has a few short routes but not a great deal, in addition the rest of the county has the occasional bridlepath. In general Cornwall is best for exploring the myriad of small lanes which are prevalent throughout the county.

Exmoor – has some good cycling and a large number of the bridlepaths are on good tracks across the moors. As with Dartmoor there is no right of access on the open moors.

South Hams – many people cite the extensive green lanes of this area as an off road cyclist's dream. Many of these routes are, however, of dubious legality. Don't be put off by this, with a bit of homework and careful map work this area has a lot to offer.

The rest of Devon also has a fair amount of potential, in particular the area between Dartmoor and Exmoor and over to the Devon/Dorset border and places such as Woodbury and Bicton commons, in East Devon.

THE ROUTE DESCRIPTIONS

The five routes, with two alternatives, contained in this book range from 'epic' trips to rather more sedate trips that the whole family can enjoy. Unless stated otherwise they can all be ridden without walking.

The time taken given for each route is the cycling time that it took me to complete the trip, NOT including any stops, in a fairly leisurely manner. Obviously if you are a fanatic, fitness-orientated rider you are going to be much faster, likewise if you want to amble along, enjoy the scenery and have a long lunch break you are going to be slower. As a general rule add a good hour to the times given to allow for planned breaks and then another half an hour to allow for unplanned stops!

The descriptions written are all going in, what was for me, the obvious direction around the route. There is nothing stopping you from riding the routes in the opposite direction. Whilst the descriptions will not be as much use to you in this case, the maps and background information will still be relevant.

The maps in this books are not designed to be used by themselves in the wilder areas, rather they are there to supplement the Ordnance Survey maps. Each sketch map has north going up the page and uses simple symbols which should be self-explanatory when read with the text. These routes all use the 1:25 000 Outdoor Leisure Series map of Dartmoor. For each route there is a grid reference for the start point, which is circled on the sketch maps. For some of the routes the ability to use a map and compass is essential whilst for others a map is a good source of secondary information. If you are not sure how to read a grid reference there is a good explanation on the margin of the OS maps. As the OS now work exclusively in kilometres, all the distances in the route descriptions are also given in kilometres and metres. Note that the sketch maps in this book are not necessarily drawn to any particular scale. Unless the route description says otherwise, always assume that the route follows the most obvious track/path continuing in the same direction.

THE COUNTRY CODE (issued by the Countryside Commission)
• Enjoy the countryside and respect its life and work
• Guard against all risks of fire
• Fasten all gates
• Keep your dogs under close control
• Keep to Public Paths across farmland
• Use gates and stiles to cross fences, hedges and walls
• Take your litter home
• Help keep all water clean
• Protect wildlife, plants and trees
• Take special care on country roads
• Make no unnecessary noise

THE OFF ROAD CODE (issued by the Mountain Bike Club)
• Only ride where you have a legal right
• Always give way to horses and walkers
• Avoid animals and crops
• Take all litter with you
• Leave all gates as found
• Keep the noise down
• Don't get annoyed with anyone, it never solves anything
• Always try to be self-sufficient, for you and your bike
• Never create a fire hazard

There is a great deal of variety on this route which travels up from Plympton on the Plym Valley Cycle Path before cutting through the line and skirting around the southern edge of the Dartmoor National Park. From here it cuts through the huge English China Clay complex at Lee Moor and the open moorland of Crownhill Down before dropping back into Plympton. Large parts of the route give dramatic views over Plymouth, the south moors and down into Cornwall. Whilst there is some rough moorland and the occasional steep hill, the route as a whole is fairly easy going and would be possible, with care, on touring bikes.

Although the cycle path proper, which the route uses, starts just below Saltram House and follows the Plym Estuary for a short way, the route is more logical if started from the large carpark of the B & Q complex on the edge of Plympton. There are however, a variety of start points that could be used.

It is well worth taking a torch for Leighbeer tunnel, although many people do not bother.

From the exit to the carpark cross the disused railway and turn right following the signpost for the cycle/foot path to Plym Valley. After 150 metres bear right at the entrance to the Royal Marine base and start on the cycle path itself, which runs between the base and the Plym Valley Railway Museum.

The cycle path is a Sustrans project, which uses the old Plymouth–Yelverton GWR railway line. This line was originally opened in 1859 by the South Devon and Tavistock Company and lasted until the widespread 'Beeching' closures of 1962. Its primary use was industrial, as can be seen by the remains of numerous slate quarries en route.

After 150 metres go through the first of a number of narrow gates on the cycle path. The Plym River joins the path on the left in another 900 metres whilst the remains of the original railway and the Cann Quarry Canal comes in from the right. 260 metres past this there is a smaller cindered track bearing off to the left.

Leave the main track and join this smaller track. 2 kilometres into the route you will pass the remains of the Plymbridge railway station before crossing the bridge over the road. This is another good access point to this route.

Here the cycle path passes through the National Trust area of Plymbridge. **Do not be tempted to leave the path to explore the many riverside trails in this area. Illegal mountain biking in the National Trust area is now becoming a real problem.** Although cyclists do technically have the right of way on the path, please do not take this too literally as the route for the next couple of kilometres is a very popular family walk, particularly at weekends. This whole valley is a stunning display of colours at most times of the year with the bluebells in spring being a particular attraction. Look out as well for the spectacular views from the high viaducts, which the path crosses. You will almost have to avoid the grey squirrels which live, seemingly in their hundreds, in the woods here. You might well also see Herons or the white and buff bobbing Dippers in the river. If you are very lucky you may even catch a glimpse of a blue Kingfisher or the black and white rump of a startled fallow deer.

4 kilometres past Plymbridge you meet the road at Bickleigh Vale. Whilst it is quite feasible to turn right here, go down the hill, turn left and rejoin the route at Shaugh Bridge. This would miss the novel attraction of Leighbeer Tunnel. The route itself turns left, goes up the short hill and then turns right at the blue sign with the cycle logo, on to Goodameavy. Incidentally the hill you have just come up figures prominently in the Commandos' training where it goes under the less than affectionate name of 'heartbreak hill'!

Shortly after rejoining the cycle path you cross the largest viaduct on the route from which you can enjoy views up the Plym Valley and across to Shaugh Prior village. 1.5 kilometres after this viaduct you reach Leighbeer tunnel which, although only 300 metres long, has a slight leftward bend. This means that from the centre point it is not possible to see either end! Try not to make the mistake to which I am prone – remove your sunglasses, it helps!

Although the track itself continues on, the permitted cycle path comes to an abrupt halt 9 kilometres into the route, i.e. just after leaving the tunnel. At the obvious sign in the tree saying 'End of Cyclepath' exit from the left side of the track. If you want to simply treat the cycle path as a day out in its own right then it is worth turning right here and, climbing the hill, make your way to the Skylark Inn in Clearbrook, which makes for a more logical turning point.

If you wish to continue, however, turn left. The number of hills which you climb over the next few kilometres are simply paying the price for coming this far, from sea level, on a virtually flat path! Exercise caution on the lanes in this area as they are a large tourist attraction, particularly at weekends when the whole population of Plymouth seems to spill out into the urban fringe area.

500 metres after leaving the cycle path turn left at the T-junction (going downhill this time!) then left again after a further 500 metres onto the Shaugh Prior road. The major tourist site of Shaugh Bridge is reached shortly after this junction. If you are lucky there is often a welcome ice cream van here. After the

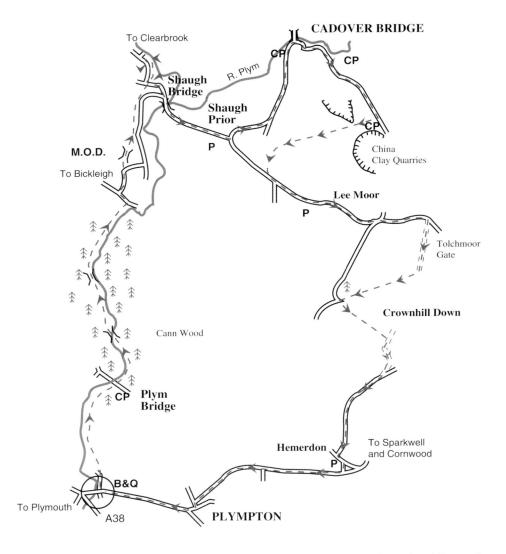

bridge you are faced with a fairly steep 500 metre long hill up into the village of Shaugh Prior itself, where you could easily be forgiven for breaking your journey in the White Thorn pub. For followers of the letterboxing pastime, which is peculiar to Dartmoor, the White Thorn is well known for its collection of 'special occasion' stamps to be collected. The village actually lies just within the south western corner of the National Park. 100 metres past the church, take the fork in the road heading left, and uphill again. In the spring and early summer the Dartmoor hedgerows such as the one you are now passing are a riot of flowers with the primroses, wild garlic and bluebells giving way to red campion, foxgloves, buttercups and brambles.

Continue up this hill until you can turn left, following signs for Cadover, at a T-junction with a more major road. 100 metres past this junction you come across one of Dartmoor's renowned stone crosses, which were originally used as waymarkers. The road you are now on forms the boundary of the National Park with the land to the left of you being in the Park and the land to the right being out of it. Directly ahead is your first glimpse of the moor with the large rock outcrop of Sheeps Tor rising up in the middle distance and the communications aerial on North Hessary Tor behind it. 1.5 kilometres after the junction you reach Cadover Bridge, according to local legend the site of a battle, Cad being the Celtic Word for conflict. Turn right just before the bridge onto the road signposted as a dead end. Once again this road marks the southern edge of the park. On the right is the first of the enormous pits of the English China Clay business, on the left are the distinctive double tops of the Trowlesworthy Tors and just in front of them Trowlesworthy Warren Farm. Where the word Warren is found on the moors it means that it was formally a site where rabbits were bred, this being the staple diet of the mining and farming communities. 2 kilometres along this road you will meet the 'Private – No Entry' signs of the E.C.C. and the old Blackaton cross.

Just before this cross, on the right side of the road, there is a small carpark, cross this and get onto the rough track (bridleway) leading between the quarries. **Keep well away from the quarries.** The open cast pit on your left was at one time reputed to be the largest man-made hole in Western Europe. 600 metres after leaving the road you come across a track crossing you at right angles, cross straight across this taking the narrow path on the left side of a small stream bed. 280 metres on cross the stream and head diagonally right up the hill, topping the rise over another track in a further 280 metres. From here head straight towards the triangulation point on Saddlesborough hill in front of you. The view from the top of this hill is well worth all the effort that it took to get here. In front of you is the remarkable panorama of Plymouth itself with the Sound laid out behind it. Farther around to the right you look over Cornwall with the distinctive cone and tower of Kit Hill being visible on a clear day. Right again and you can see in the distance the famous church of St Michael perched high on the volcanic core of Brent Tor, and finally right of that are the southern moors. From the hill top take the small path which heads directly towards the large bay of Plymouth Sound.

The earthworks that you are now passing are not as might be supposed the remains of mining but rather the remains of a far older village settlement. 50 metres down from the hill top you cross a distinctive boundary earth wall. Continue down the left side of another earthwork boundary still in the direction of Plymouth Sound. Head just to the right of the obvious rocks of Hawks Tor where you come across a more distinct track heading in the same direction. Stay on this track heading downhill to the left of the small wood in front of you. After meeting the road turn left towards the Moorlands Hotel. Stay on this modern road, which bypasses the old mining villages of Wotter and Lee Moor, ignoring all the turns, for 3.6 kilometres.

After this distance you will reach Tolchmoor Gate on the right side of the road.

This gate is marked by a large sign reading 'No vehicular access – bridleway only'. Before you go through the gate take time to look at the large block of stone on the left side of the road with the square hole in it which once held a barrier, possibly for some sort of toll road. Once through the gate, remember to close it, and keep on the track heading gently downhill. 340 metres down the track it seems to disappear, so look diagonally up to your left and you will see where it continues heading towards a gate on the top of the hill. After this gate, marked entrance, take the track heading down to your right to where it drops into a small valley. Here you will come across yet another gate, this time complete with stile. Cross this and take the path directly in front of you, carry on downhill for 100 metres until just after the path goes through a water run off. Here the path veers to the left and contours around the hill keeping at a constant height. Continue like this for 600 metres until you come around the front of the hill crossing a whole mishmash of tracks. In front of you, at the bottom of the valley, is the green/white water of the china clay settling tanks. Just to the left of these there is a small triangular shaped wood. Head downhill across semi-open moorland, to the left hand corner of this wood. At the wood follow the track along its left hand side until it reaches the road. Here there are a number of tracks heading left, the one you want is the furthest left going back at a right angle to the one you have just come in on. This new track continues, gently uphill, for just over a kilometre where it meets a number of other paths. Ignore these and continue straight on for another 500 metres. Here you meet a large, white track crossing your front. Turn right on this track and follow it for 200 metres until it meets the corner of a small wood. Turn left here, keeping to the edge of the wood heading downhill. Shortly down the hill you come across another large, white track, turn right onto it and you should be facing the remains of the old Hemerdon Ball mine workings on the hill in front of you. At one time this mine was a major producer of Titanium and Arsenic. Stay on this track now until you reach Drakelands Farm where you cross a small ford and join a small country lane.

Keeping on this road for a little over a kilometre will bring you into the small village of Hemerdon. The main attraction of this village is the excellent Miner's Arms pub! After the pub follow the road around to the right, ignoring the left fork until, after another 100 metres, you come to a T-junction. Turn right, heading downhill and following the sign for Plympton, but be warned this narrow lane can be very busy at times. When you come to a small roundabout at the bottom of the hill keep to the right following signs for Colebrook. Stay on the road through the village until, after a kilometre, you come to a T-junction with a railway bridge on your left. Turn left, over the bridge and then immediately right and right again at the two mini roundabouts. You are now stuck on this main road for 2 kilometres. Just before you reach Marsh Mills roundabout you cross a small humpbacked bridge, immediately after which take a sharp left at the yellow cycle diversion sign. Then after 100 metres turn left, back onto the original cycle path which takes you under the main road you have just left and back to the start of the route.

ROUTE TWO: PRINCETOWN

Burrator, Sheepstor, Ditsworthy Warren House, Nun's Cross, Princetown, Routrundle Farm.
Distance: 25.6 km/15.9 miles (7.65 km on road)
Time: 3 hours
Start: SX 551 680
Maps: 1:25 000 Leisure Series No 28, Dartmoor

This route is a good introduction to southern Dartmoor. It includes a variety of terrain but is generally on rough moorland tracks. There is a bit of hill climbing to be done and as a result the route is fairly demanding. The circuit passes a number of old farms as well as two particularly spectacular standing stones and the oldest cross on Dartmoor. In addition you will also travel through the remains of a large tin mining complex, granite quarries and the Princetown railway. Finally there is Princetown and the infamous prison itself.

The route starts at the western end of the Burrator Dam. This is a very popular weekend location and as a result is well served with parking, public toilets and of

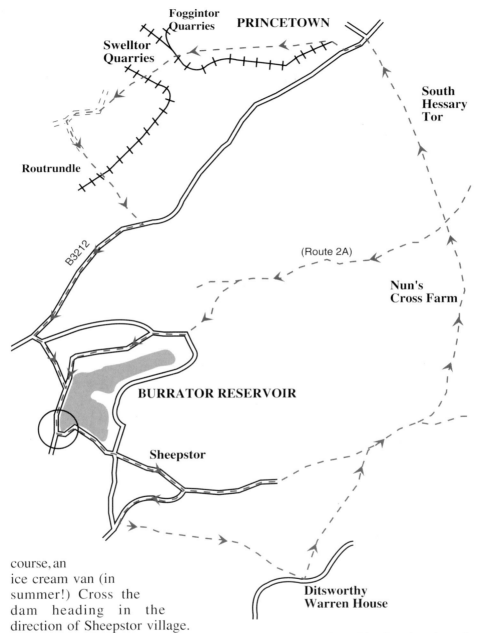

Foggintor Quarries

PRINCETOWN

Swelltor Quarries

South Hessary Tor

Routrundle

B3212

(Route 2A)

Nun's Cross Farm

BURRATOR RESERVOIR

Sheepstor

Ditsworthy Warren House

course, an ice cream van (in summer!) Cross the dam heading in the direction of Sheepstor village.

The main attractions of this tiny village are both to be found in the churchyard. Buried here are the three White Rajah Brookes of Sarawak, in Borneo, who came from these parts. You will also find the remains of the old bear-baiting pit, at one time a common entertainment. Note that, unusually, Sheepstor has no pub and no village shop. Stay on the road right through the village and you will soon start to climb the 500 metre long hill. Near the top of the hill the road curls sharply around to the right from where there are good views over the village and up to Sheepstor itself. The wall that you pass on the right side is typical of the 'deer leap' style of wall found on the moors. Steep on the outside and usually with a ditch as well they are inclined on the inside, this is in order to ensure that no deer remained trapped in the fields in the days when Dartmoor was a hunting reserve and deer were the sole property of the king!

After 3.25 kilometres on the road a track appears on the left. If you start to head downhill towards a building enclosed by trees you have gone too far! Take this track and after 170 metres you come to a gate with a signpost saying 'Public Bridlepath – Ditsworthy Warren House 1½ miles'. Through the gate and straight ahead there is a sandy track which soon gives way to a rough moorland path. Follow this for 340 metres to the brow of the hill in front of you. Legis Tor is immediately in front with the Trowlesworthy Tors on the hill behind and English China Clay workings away to the right. Don't take the obvious route going straight on. The track bears away to the left here heading towards a small hill. 540 metres farther on the track veers slightly to the right dropping down a small dip and then up again keeping the hill, which is in fact Gutter Tor, on the left. If you have got it right the mass of Hen Tor, just below the skyline on the other side of the valley, should be directly in front of you. Another gate is reached after a further 800 metres. This one is signposted back to Ringmoor Cottage, where you left the road.

Head towards the obvious building at the end of the track in front of you. This is Ditsworthy Warren House with the fledgling River Plym flowing below it. As you approach it you are cycling over layers of history. Note the old earthworks and the 'pillow mounds' or artificial rabbit warren which gave the building its name. Despite its deserted appearance, the farm is actually used by the armed forces as a base for outdoor activities. If it is not being used it is well worth while having a look around the grounds. In particular go into the large enclosure behind the farm and look for the three potato caves built into the walls, these being the forerunners of today's fridge! It is always interesting to speculate how many Neolithic and Bronze age remains were uprooted and used in the construction of centuries old farms such as this one.

Leave the farm on the large obvious track just to the left and rear of the farmhouse as you approached it. The spoil tips down to your right in the Plym valley are the typical remains of early tin mining. 400 metres along you need to leave the track. In front of you are two large and impressive standing stones, just to the left of which is the small Drizzlecombe valley. Take a direct line across the moor, to the left hand bank of this valley. As you approach the valley you will find a small rough path going slightly uphill on its left edge. This whole area is alive with history, earth works, hut circles, pounds and, on your right, the stone row in which are the two standing stones you saw earlier. The larger of these is in fact one of the largest standing stones on the moors. Just over a kilometre after leaving the track at Ditsworthy you start to come across the low remains of the Eylesbarrow tin mine, at one time a large and thriving complex. At the top of the Drizzlecombe valley go across the first track which crosses the route. 140 metres farther on a much larger sandy track joins you from the left. Take this track, also going slightly uphill, carrying on in the same direction i.e. bearing right. From here enjoy the spectacular views to the left over the Burrator valley. 650 metres up this track, ignore the right fork and continue uphill in the same direction. The track here winds around the remains of old shafts, although they are all filled in in this area it is always a good idea to treat them with a little caution. Stick to the obvious sandy track, which bends to the left through the shafts, and you soon come over the hill onto a wider track heading downhill. There is a great temptation here to go hell for leather down this fast part of the route. Be warned, however, there is the occasional stony surprise for the unwary rider! Also avoid leaving the track here to ride on the open moor – if too many people do this there will soon be a 20-metre wide scar on the hillside.

Nearer the bottom of the hill do not take the track veering off right to the farmhouse but stay straight on down the hill on the track which takes you to the cross itself. This is Nun's Cross or, to give it its original name, Siward's Cross. Although much about it is mystery, it is in fact widely believed to be the oldest of Dartmoor's stone crosses. The obvious, and somewhat clumsy, restoration of the cross took place in 1846.

NB: The path in the next section has undergone extensive renovation, which includes the use of drainage ditches. Please do not go around the ends of these ditches as this only causes erosion on an even wider scale.

Continue on from Nun's Cross in the same direction on the same sandy path. After 900 metres the path comes to a large cross roads with a nearby boundary stone. This is the junction at which you would turn left if taking the shorter route described in Route 2A. The present route, which is shortly joined by a wall coming in from the right, continues straight across the junction heading for the small rocky outcrop of South Hessary Tor on top of the small rise in front. After the tor the path, still with the wall on the right, drops down into Princetown. Note that this part of the path can be very boggy in places and also well churned up because of its proximity to the road. Please avoid adding to this erosion.

Princetown is well worth a stop, not least for its unsavoury history. It is rumoured that the prison was built on land given by the Prince of Wales (hence the name) as 'the bleakest place in all the kingdom'. Graves of the many French and American prisoners who didn't survive their stay here can be found in the churchyard. There are a number of good pubs and cafes in Princetown, the Plume of Feathers in particular being very well known. This pub also offers very good bunk house style accommodation. The High Dartmoor Interpretation Centre is also worth a visit.

From the track that brought you into Princetown turn left onto the road. Stay on this road for just over 300 metres. Over a cattle grid and immediately past a pair of buildings at the entrance to the town, turn right onto a small, rough track.

This track takes you down to the left hand corner of a small wood. Despite all appearances the route does not follow the obvious disused railway, which is not a bridleway. Turn right up the edge of the wood towards the large aerial of North Hessary Tor. Follow this edge for 20 metres and then bear left onto a very rough moorland path. Stay on this path, which may mean walking at times. After a short climb you should be staying roughly parallel to the railway track 100 metres or so down to the left. The path, which is a bridleway, is virtually nonexistent for much of its length. If you reach the top of the hill and find yourself facing the large disused quarry and lake of Foggintor you have gone too far to the right. 2.25 kilometres after leaving the railway you should rejoin it at a large track junction. Turn left here on a large surfaced track heading downhill towards the corner of a wall. Here the track bends around to the left following the wall, the route however, continues in across the moor skirting around to the left of the spoil tips of Swelltor quarries. The quarries in this area at one time produced much of the granite facing stone used in this country. Many of the major buildings in London are faced with Dartmoor granite.

After a short distance you yet again cross the railway, this time look for the bridleway sign pointing through a small gap in the wall. Go through this gate and follow the path which drops steeply downhill and is too rough to cycle. After this initial steep drop the path evens out and is well marked with blue discs on the rocks every few metres. On the whole this is a delightful path crossing through an area of stunted Hawthorn trees. 600 metres on this path brings you to a main track where you turn left, away from Criptor farm. At the gate which you pass after a short distance, look to your right along the direction of the wall and half way up the hill on the other side of the valley, The large outcrop is Vixen Tor. This tor is not only the tallest slab of rock on the moor it is also reputed to be the home of the witch Vixana who lured travellers to their deaths in the surrounding bogs.

Our route however continues on the same track until you meet the head of the road. Turn left here onto another large, well surfaced track marked 'Farm Access only – Routrundle Farm'. Stay on this track, through a gate and past the idyllic longhouse building of Routrundle Farm itself where the track reverts to a green path for a short distance before, yet again, crossing the railway. Cross the railway, going straight ahead uphill on the moorland track. Turn right where you meet the road at a small carpark and continue uphill.

Just when you might start to think that the whole route is uphill, the road crosses the brow of the hill, the panorama of the Tamar Valley opens out in front of you and the road takes off downhill. Don't, however, get too carried away because after 2.25 kilometres the road comes to a crossroads where you take a very sharp left turn. Try and get a glimpse of the small cross in the hedge on your left but reserve your energy for the final, brutal, 250 metre hill. Just after entering the woods at the brow of the hill there is a road forking left. Take this road, turning left at the bottom, if you want a last final fling around Burrator reservoir. Otherwise stay on the road straight ahead, enjoy the long run down through the woods, turn right at the bottom and you are shortly back at the start of the route.

The view from the top of Sheeps Tor, looking towards Leather Tor and Sharpitor, with the eastern end of Burrator Reservoir down below.

ROUTE 2A: CRAZY WELL POOL

Length: 6.5 km/4 miles (link only)
 18.2 km/11.3 miles (in total)

A good shorter version of Route two can be made by turning left at the track junction following Nun's Cross 11.67 kilometres into that route. This track, which is downhill almost all the way, is broad and reasonably well surfaced crossing the small Older Bridge after about 500 metres. Just short of 2 kilometres past this there is an earth cutting and small stream leading up to the right. This leads to Crazy Well Pool (no bridleway access but only about 200 metres from the track) one of the most legend-bound spots on the moor. Amongst these are the stories that the pool was once the home of the witch of Sheepstor, that the pool is bottomless and that its level goes up and down with the tide at Plymouth. In reality the pool is probably a tin miners reservoir of about the sixteenth century.

Shortly after the cutting leading to the pool, the track enters an area of forestry. When a large junction is reached, keep to the route heading down and left. This brings you down to the road. Turn right here and follow the road around Burrator Reservoir until you come back to the dam.

ROUTE THREE: GRIMSPOUND

Hound Tor, Jay's Grave, Grimspound, Warren House Inn, Coombe Down, Easdon, Manaton, Bowerman's Nose.
Distance: 20.5 km/12.7 miles (9.7 km on road)
Time: 3½ hours
Start: SX 739 792
Maps: 1:25 000 Leisure Series No 28, Dartmoor

This route takes in some of the most famous legends on Dartmoor, it also includes a wide variety of spectacular moorland scenery from open moorland to small farms. It is a demanding route that should not be taken lightly, the challenge for the off-road freak will be to stay on the bike for as long as possible. Saner people will find that there are a number of ascents and descents which will be better done on foot!

Start the route at the large carpark below Hound Tor. There is a deservedly popular tea-van here on all but midweek winter days. From the carpark entrance turn right, right again and then take the left fork which is signposted by a small wooden sign to 'Jay's Grave 800 yds'. The grave itself is met at 890 metres from the start of the route. The story of Jay's grave appears to be founded on fact although there is discrepancy about the name, which is either Kitty Jay or Mary Jay. Either way it seems certain that she was a young workhouse girl employed at a farm near Manaton where she was seduced by the son of the house. In despair she committed suicide and as a result was buried not in consecrated land but at a crossroads on the parish boundaries to prevent the devil claiming her spirit and to prevent her finding her way back to the parish to haunt the living. This sad story is made all the more poignant by the fresh flowers which are always left on her grave, although no one has ever admitted to putting them there.

Turn left here, through the five-barred gate behind the gate onto the bridlepath signposted to Natsworthy Gate. This generally well surfaced track brings you out onto a small road after 1.17 km, turn left and then immediately right following the bridlepath sign to Firth Bridge. Cross the small stream and follow the broad path along the edge of the wood. After 440 metres stay on the major track which starts to climb away left from the wood. Stick to the obvious track heading uphill. Another 430 metres brings you to a large standing stone, which records the crash of an RAF aircraft returning from action in 1941 in which all the crew perished. Full details of the incident are given on a slate plaque set into the rear of the stone. From the memorial stone turn around and retrace your route for 50 metres and turn left at the track crossroads heading slightly uphill. The poles sticking up to your left were, believe it or not, to prevent enemy gliders from landing in the Second World War! The top of the hill is met shortly after this junction and you descend

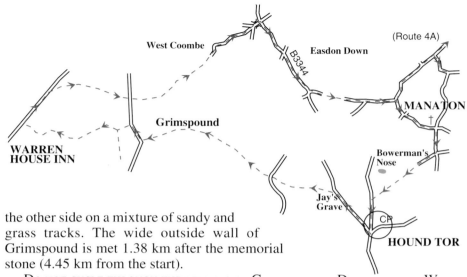

the other side on a mixture of sandy and grass tracks. The wide outside wall of Grimspound is met 1.38 km after the memorial stone (4.45 km from the start).

DO NOT CYCLE THROUGH THE REMAINS OF GRIMSPOUND—DISMOUNT AND WALK.

Grimspound is the best known prehistoric site on Dartmoor, dating from the Bronze/Iron age of about 3,000 years ago. It would at one time have been a thriving community of 24 huts. The wide walls were not for defence – these were peaceful people – but to keep wild animals out and their own livestock in. The centre hut has been largely reconstructed as has the main entrance to your left. Walk straight across the side and leave just to the right of a small stream. From this paved exit the white building just below the skyline in the distance ahead of you is the Warren House Inn, towards which you are heading. Follow the path down to the right, crossing the stream and heading for the road in the dip. Turn right, uphill, for about 400 metres. On your left are some deep gullies from the days of tin mining on the moor, which dominate the landscape for the next mile or two. At the top of these workings there is an unsigned bridlepath, in the shape of a green corridor, heading off to the left downhill. It leads down to a point behind Headland Warren, a farm that does Bed & Breakfast now but was once a pub patronised by the tin miners of the locality. It was then known as the Birch Tor Inn. Near it is a signpost pointing you onwards in the direction of the Warren House Inn.

After a hundred metres or so you come to the top of the short climb. Just to your left is the first of the cuttings of the Vitifer Mine complex, look behind that for a good example of a multiple stone row. The stony path now descends for 820 metres (7.21 km from start) to the remains of some buildings. This is all that is left of the Vitifer Mine working, once a very important site for tin production. Although the mine ceased real output in the last century, tin ore was extracted from the mine remains as late as 1939 making this the last tin taken from Dartmoor. Cross the small stream on the granite slabs and climb the short hill beyond, again following the line of the telegraph poles. This rough path soon reaches a broad well surfaced track. Ignore the left fork and stay on the main track until it reaches the road. The Warren House Inn is 200 metres or so up to your left.

There are as many legends about this inn as almost any site on Dartmoor. The Inn is actually a building that was moved from a site on the lower side of the road. Like all buildings with the name Warren it was originally a warrener's house for breeding rabbits – the tinners' symbol of three linked rabbits is above the door. The fire inside the inn has never been allowed to go out, indeed it was carried over from the original building. The most famous legend in the area concerns one Jan Reynolds who was spotted by the Devil playing cards in Widecombe Church. The Devil promptly carried him away, tearing the pinnacle of the church off in the process. As the unfortunate Jan Reynolds was carried over the Warren House Inn he dropped his cards. It is reckoned that the shapes of the four suits can be seen in the shapes of the cattle pounds visible from the Inn, although I have never managed it. Once again this is a story based on fact, as the church at Widecombe was in fact damaged by a violent storm in 1638 and a number of people in the church at the time lost their lives.

From the Inn go back to where you joined the road and continue on for another 650 metres to the car park at Bennett's Cross. Little is known of this cross, which is of medieval origin, although it may possibly be a marker on the route from Chagford to Tavistock. The route you want here is not the recently reconstructed path which heads up to Birch Tor but the path which runs almost parallel to the road before curving away to the right behind the tor. This path continues slightly uphill, crossing innumerable drainage ditches for some 700 metres. The top is marked by a curious hut/mound-shaped structure. Just beyond this is a small crossroads over which you go straight across and start down the hill on the other side. To the left and behind you from here you look over the north moors with Fernworthy reservoir in the foreground. In front of you, slightly to the right, is the distinctive circular shape of Grimspound. Follow the path down to where it crosses the road at the point where an obvious wall comes down the hill in front of you to join it. The path then follows the left side of this wall for 380 metres (10.65 km from start) to a wall junction. Turn left here, following the wall to a five-barred gate. Going through the gate the route goes downhill diagonally left heading towards a small reservoir in the dip at the bottom of the hill. This is Coombe Down and contains a number of large prehistoric hut circles. The town in the distance, in front of you, is Moretonhampstead. At the reservoir take the track, through mixed woodland, keeping to the left of the stream as you descend. This track soon becomes a semi-tarmaced road continuing to the farm of West Coombe. Note the sign regarding a 'small brown dog'! Going through the gate, continue straight through the farm passing a curious beehive-shaped building at the farm exit. This track soon bears around to the right and turns into a minor road. Ignore the right turning by the stream, and continue on the road until you reach a T-junction 1.2 km from the farm. Turn right here and continue on this B-road following the sign to Manaton for another 1.6 km (14.94 km from start) and turn left at the junction marked Easdon Cottage. This road curls around in front of the farm and soon becomes a narrow path. Continue straight on keeping the wall on your right until reaching a metal gate after 500 metres. The view to your right here is one of the finest I have seen from anywhere in Dartmoor with Haytor the obvious double monoliths in the distance, Hound Tor the jagged hill in front of that, Honeybag and Chinkwell Tors to the right and Hayne Down nearest to you.

Go through the metal gate and back onto a minor road, then follow this to a T-junction with a B-road. Stay on this road, around the right hand bend (if you are

doing Routes 3 and 4 combined go straight on at this bend to Langstone), following signs for Manaton. You reach the idyllic village green and church at Manaton after a little over 1.5 km on this road. Turn right here down the small road marked unsuitable for wide vehicles and signposted to Leighon. After 540 metres on this minor road you come to a crossroads at Sandy Meadow. Turn right here, following the bridlepath signs to Hayne Down, Jay's Grave and Natsworthy Gate. Another 260 metres brings you onto a small gravelled path which bears around to the left in front of the house called Hayne. This path soon becomes a trudge up a 300 metre long steep hill. Take either path at the fork after 100 metres, the left path is probably the better of the two. As the path breaks out onto more open moorland head uphill keeping any path which takes you to the left of the obvious tor on the skyline in front of you. At the top of the hill you should be on a saddle in between two unnamed tors. The large monolith of rock known as Bowerman's Nose is in front of the right hand of these tors. (You will need to leave your bikes as it is a couple of hundred metres off the bridlepath.) Bowerman's Nose is, in legend, the remains of a local hunter turned to stone by a powerful witch for disturbing a witch's coven whilst out hunting. Likewise Hound Tor is supposed to be Bowerman's pack, also turned to stone at the same time. Continuing on down the hill, head towards the point at which a metal gate crosses the minor road in front of you. Go through this gate, i.e. turn left on the road and after 880 metres you come to the thatched house at Swallerton Gate. Turn left and left again and you are back at the car park (and tea van) where you started below Hound Tor.

ROUTE FOUR: LUSTLEIGH CLEAVE

Water, Manaton, Foxworthy Bridge, Hunter's Tor, Sharpitor, Hisley Bridge.
Distance: 13.8 km/8.6 miles (3 km on road)
Time: 3 hours
Start: SX 785 793
Maps: 1:25 000 Leisure Series No 28, Dartmoor

This route explores another side to Dartmoor with its tiny hidden hamlets, steep valleys and wooded pathways. Lustleigh Cleave was one of the original tourist destinations of the charabanc tours from bygone years. It is probably a route better suited to those with an inclination to exploration rather than speed – in a number of places it is necessary to dismount and walk. Owing to this and the number of short steep hills that the route includes it is rather a strenuous day out. It is worthwhile doing the route in winter when the bramble and gorse bushes will have died back, otherwise you finish up feeling like a pin cushion. There are no pubs or shops en route.

The start of the route is down the small tarmaced road marked "Not Suitable for Vehicles" on the outside of a sharp right-angled bend on the main Manaton – Bovey Tracey road. Go 50 metres past the road junction and there is a sizeable carpark on the right (coming from Bovey Tracey). It is well worthwhile looking at the view from this carpark. The large wooded valley in front of you is Lustleigh Cleave with the River Bovey at its bottom. Your route crosses this valley twice, although at its lower points! The high point at the far right end of the valley is Hunter's Tor, which is also the high point of the route.

The minor road, which is in fact the 'old Manaton road', on which the route starts is only tarmaced for a short distance. As you go down the hill it becomes progressively more broken until, after 500 metres, there is no trace of tarmac left. Follow the well-surfaced track, which continues on, forward through some beautiful woodland, bearing left at the fork at 950 metres from the start. You should be following signposts marked 'Bridlepath to Manaton'. After another 1.15 kilometres, and shortly after crossing the small Becka Brook (the famous tourist spot of 'Becky Falls' is a couple of kilometres up stream from here), the track starts to decay and the first of the day's climbs really starts. Bend around to the right at the fork as the track comes around on itself. Another 470 metres brings you to another junction – this time go straight across the crossroads. The track actually bends to the right, once again following bridlepath signs to Manaton. You will be relieved to hear that the top of the hill is just around the next corner! 300 metres on from the junction you meet a short section of tarmaced road, which takes you slightly downhill again!

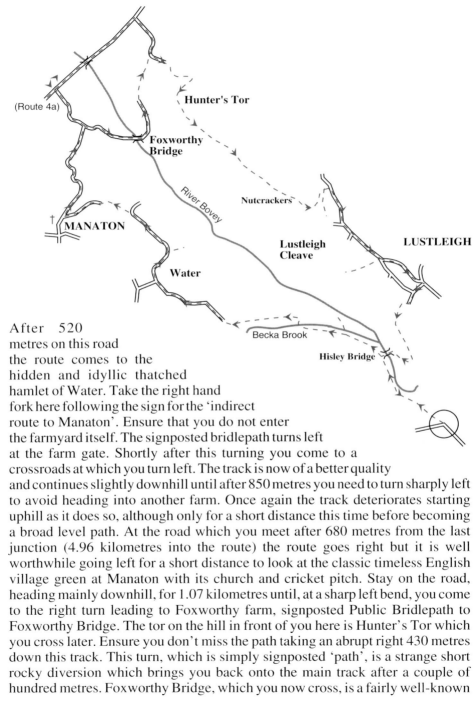

(Route 4a)

Hunter's Tor

Foxworthy
Bridge

River Bovey

Nutcrackers

† MANATON

Lustleigh
Cleave

LUSTLEIGH

Water

Becka Brook

Hisley Bridge

After 520 metres on this road the route comes to the hidden and idyllic thatched hamlet of Water. Take the right hand fork here following the sign for the 'indirect route to Manaton'. Ensure that you do not enter the farmyard itself. The signposted bridlepath turns left at the farm gate. Shortly after this turning you come to a crossroads at which you turn left. The track is now of a better quality and continues slightly downhill until after 850 metres you need to turn sharply left to avoid heading into another farm. Once again the track deteriorates starting uphill as it does so, although only for a short distance this time before becoming a broad level path. At the road which you meet after 680 metres from the last junction (4.96 kilometres into the route) the route goes right but it is well worthwhile going left for a short distance to look at the classic timeless English village green at Manaton with its church and cricket pitch. Stay on the road, heading mainly downhill, for 1.07 kilometres until, at a sharp left bend, you come to the right turn leading to Foxworthy farm, signposted Public Bridlepath to Foxworthy Bridge. The tor on the hill in front of you here is Hunter's Tor which you cross later. Ensure you don't miss the path taking an abrupt right 430 metres down this track. This turn, which is simply signposted 'path', is a strange short rocky diversion which brings you back onto the main track after a couple of hundred metres. Foxworthy Bridge, which you now cross, is a fairly well-known beauty spot and once again is overwhelmingly idyllic. This is actually the top end of Lustleigh Cleave. At the buildings, which contain as good an example of barn conversion as you're likely to see, turn left following public bridlepath signs to 'Peck Farm'. Immediately after leaving the buildings follow the blue arrow which takes you right onto yet another loose, stony uphill path. Turn right again at the semi-tarmaced junction which you soon reach. There is a sign here, for Hammerslake, although it is quite well hidden in the hedge.

Shortly after this junction you come to Peck Farm. Don't go into the farm itself, the route goes straight ahead through the five-bar gate which has the bridlepath sign on the top bar. Follow the uphill path on the left edge of the rough ground until you reach a path sign taking you sharply right. From here the views start to become more dramatic until at the top of Hunter's Tor they become simply stunning. Away to your right and behind you are the settlements of North Bovey and Moretonhampstead. It is the view in front that counts, however. If you stop by the gate (640 metres from Peck Farm and 8.15 kilometres into the route) the large double monolith on the skyline in front of you is Haytor. Staying on the skyline right of that is the castellated tops of Hound Tor and right again is the single pillar of Bowerman's Nose. These are three of Dartmoor's best known landmarks (see Route Three). To your left are the remains of a hill fort of Roman origin, possibly earlier, which if the bracken is high can be quite hard to see. Another local legend has it that this spot is haunted by the ghosts of Roman legionnaires locked in combat with their Celtic enemies. Having said that, this is a wonderful spot for a lunch break!

The path on from here follows the top edge of the Cleave (actually a corruption of the old Celtic word for cliff). You should be on a fairly broad well surfaced path, if not hunt around a little bit as there are a number of paths heading in the same vague direction. Avoid the path which forks off left into the site of the fort. After a kilometre or so on this path the descent starts to get to the point where it is necessary to dismount and walk. 50 metres into the descent you arrive at Sharpitor, a large group of rocks which includes the logan stone known as the 'Nut Crackers' supposedly because local people used to crack nuts under this rocking or logging stone! Whether you have any nuts with you or not it is well worth climbing out onto the far high point of the tor as the view from here is particularly rewarding. Ignore the gate on the left which is met after another 580 metres down the descent. Continue down the narrow path, turning right here, until you meet a signposted path junction. Go through the small five-barred gate in front of you and after a short distance in a typical Devon sunken path you come to a minor road. Turn right here and after a while the road drops downhill. The first bridlepath you come to after 900 metres is not the one you want, the correct path is met immediately after passing a road coming in from the left after another 530 metres. This path, which is signposted public bridlepath to Bovey Valley and Hisley Bridge, takes you up to and then, following the signs, around the farm of Lower Hisley.

The descending kilometre long path which follows shortly after the farm is a good place to blow away the cobwebs and any frustrations you may have from the previous paths. Be warned, however, that there is a rocky bend halfway down! At the junction with the large footpath to Lustleigh turn sharply left and down to Hisley Bridge which takes you across the River Bovey at the bottom end of the Cleave. Just after the bridge there is another junction, which is in fact back on the old Manaton Road. Turn left and you will soon find yourself on the final leg-straining climb back up the broken tarmac to the start of the route.

The River Bovey in Lustleigh Cleave

ROUTE 4A: ROUTES 3 AND 4 COMBINED

Although Routes three and four come very close to each other they have been treated as separate routes both because of their lengths and their very different characters. It is, however, quite feasible to combine the two routes to make an excellent, full, and strenuous, day out.

Perhaps the best way to do this is to start as for Route four. On reaching Manaton cycle past the church and straight across the crossroads onto the minor road signposted to Leighon, thus taking you on to Route three. On the return, after joining the B road after Easdon go straight on to Langstone at the sharp right hand bend, follow this road downhill for one km, turn right to Neadon and after 480 metres you come to the left turn for Foxworthy Bridge back onto Route four. Alternatively ignore the right turn for Neadon, continue on across the river and take the next right to Peck Farm which also brings you onto the route.

Doing the route in this way gives good breaks at Hound Tor carpark and the Warren House Inn.

ROUTE FIVE: HARFORD MOOR

Ivybridge, Stowford Moor Gate, Weatherdon Hill, Hangershell Rock, Harford Moor Gate, Harford Cross.
Distance: 10.58 km/6.6 miles (5.5 km on road)
Time: 1¹/₄ hours
Start: SX 636 563
Maps: 1: 25 000 Leisure Series No 28, Dartmoor.

This route is great for a short blast if you live near Ivybridge. It is a route which takes in some good, fast, open moorland riding without having to ride miles to get to it. Although I have done this route in appalling weather, it does involve some tricky route finding so it is best done in good visibility.

Start at the carpark, in Harford Road, just after the High Street through Ivybridge crosses the River Erme. The junction is signposted to the Parish Church, Health Centre and Community College. The large yellow building here is the now defunct but once important coaching inn 'The London Hotel'. Going up Harford Road you pass the Ivy Bridge on your left. Legend has it that the town is named after this bridge which until 1823 carried the main highway out of Plymouth. The next landmark on your left is the Stowford Paper Mill, one of the original industries of the town. A short steep hill takes you past the Community College, keep going until you reach a staggered junction 780 metres from the start. Go straight across the junction, crossing the railway bridge and entering the Dartmoor National Park. Another 270 metres brings you to a track going off on the right signposted 'Public Bridlepath to Moor'. Take this track, following it around to the left and through a five-barred gate. The track in front of you is an old drover's road which has existed since medieval times. It not only gets progressively steeper but also gets looser and should defeat most attempts to stay in the saddle!

Happily it is only 830 metres before you come to the five-barred gate of Stowford Moor Gate which opens onto the open moor. Spare the time to look at the huge deer leap walls on either side of you here (see Route two for explanation) the rough ground in front of you is the result of nineteenth century tin mining. The path on from here is a little confusing. Do not take the large green path which goes up diagonally right. The path you want is a smaller one which goes up the hill less steeply just to the right of the rough ground and continuing in almost the same direction as the track you have just left. 880 metres on this path brings you to the disused 'Puffing Billy' track (2.76 km from start) which carried china clay from the Red Lake workings from 1910 to 1932. Despite being one of the most popular cycling routes on Dartmoor, the track is not a legal right of way and is not likely to be one in the near future either. The route continues straight across the track

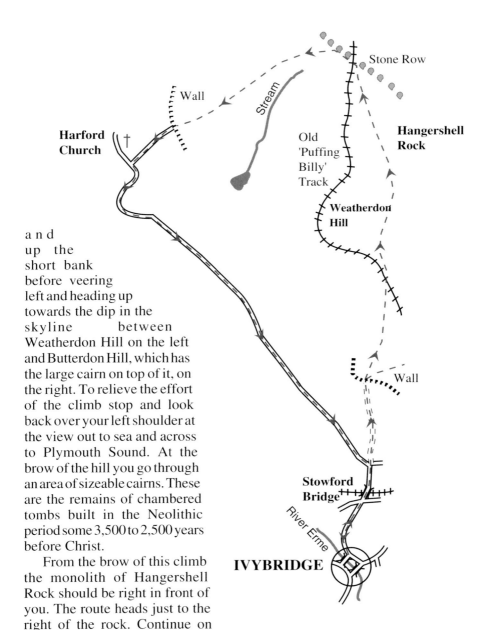

Harford Church

Wall

Stream

Old 'Puffing Billy' Track

Stone Row

Hangershell Rock

Weatherdon Hill

Wall

Stowford Bridge

River Erme

IVYBRIDGE

a n d up the short bank before veering left and heading up towards the dip in the skyline between Weatherdon Hill on the left and Butterdon Hill, which has the large cairn on top of it, on the right. To relieve the effort of the climb stop and look back over your left shoulder at the view out to sea and across to Plymouth Sound. At the brow of the hill you go through an area of sizeable cairns. These are the remains of chambered tombs built in the Neolithic period some 3,500 to 2,500 years before Christ.

From the brow of this climb the monolith of Hangershell Rock should be right in front of you. The route heads just to the right of the rock. Continue on past the rock in the same direction and the line of a stone row soon comes into view on your right. Once you see this row head for the point at which it crosses the 'Puffing Billy' track, which has come back into view on the left. Once again go straight across the track. As you do so take note of two woods in front of you. The one on the left contains a small reservoir with the second one on the right being a bit farther away. Follow the line of the stone row for 200 metres until a slightly larger flat sided stone is met, turn left here and cross about 1.5 km of open moorland. Keep high on the right side of the stream heading for a spot which is about one third of the way from the reservoir wood to the right hand wood. If you maintain your height there should be no problem and as you cross the brow of the hill there is a good run down to the carpark at Harford Moor Gate (6.12 km from start).

Get onto the small lane which takes you swiftly downhill to the picturesque church at Harford Cross. Turn left here. Apart from a couple of easy uphill stretches the road heads straight down, and fast, back to Ivybridge. You pass the original turn onto the moor after 2.9 km (9.58 km from start) continue on, retracing the route across the staggered junction back down to the carpark at the London Hotel.

DIARY OF A DARTMOOR WALKER, CHIPS BARBER
This light-hearted book includes many unusual strolls, rambles, excursions, expeditions, safaris, pilgrimages and explorations into all areas of the Dartmoor National Park. The 'diary' spans the four seasons to provide Dartmoor enthusiasts with a splendid portfolio of drawings, photographs and three-dimensional profiles that capture Dartmoor in a way that no other book has managed so far – and the walks are quite interesting too!

THE GREAT WALKS OF DARTMOOR, TERRY BOUND
This book is a 'must' for any serious Dartmoor walker! It features all the classic long walks that Dartmoor offers including the Abbots' Way, Lich Way, OATS walk, Dartmoor Perambulation, Mariners' Way and the Ten Tors.

DARTMOOR IN COLOUR, CHIPS BARBER
Dartmoor is a land often described as England's last great wilderness and there are remote tracts of land where you can wander for miles without seeing another person. In contrast, within Dartmoor's 365 square miles there are popular places where crowds are drawn to savour Dartmoor's unique atmosphere. Chips Barber has compiled over 50 colourful photos to create a lasting souvenir of this magnificent and inspiring landscape.

TEN FAMILY WALKS ON DARTMOOR, SALLY/CHIPS BARBER
Designed for the visitor to Dartmoor who wants to get away from it all for just a few hours, here is a series of sensible strolls that are interesting, with clear but simple maps, revealing the most beautiful parts of Dartmoor. The walks range from just a few miles up to about 6 or 7 miles in length, all presented in a light and easy-to-read style.

THE A TO Z OF DARTMOOR TORS, TERRY BOUND
Terry Bound probably knows Dartmoor better than any other living author and he has compiled this definitive guide to all the Dartmoor Tors. He has visited nearly every known and unknown tor on and around the moor and uses his considerable knowledge to identify other landmarks and distinguishing features. With this invaluable guide on their bookshelves, no Dartmoor enthusiast need ever again be in any doubt as to the identity or location of any Tor.

THE TEMPLER WAY, DEREK BEAVIS
Derek Beavis has put together a first class guide to The Templer Way, one which gives you the option of following it in short, simple stages or, if you are person enough, one long safari. The story of the Haytor Granite Tramway and the Stover Canal are but two of many historic features along the route which are fully described. Packed with maps and some splendid photographs, this book is the perfect guide to the Templer way.

WALKS IN THE SHADOW OF DARTMOOR, DENIS MCCALLUM
Denis McCallum has always been a keen walker but it is only since his retirement that he has fully explored this area round the edge of Dartmoor, thus discovering many little-used paths and byways in this glorious countryside. The result of his explorations is this book of ten walks – all in the Shadow of Dartmoor.

These are just a few of the many books we publish on Dartmoor, Devon and the West Country. For further details please contact us at 2 Church Hill, Pinhoe, Exeter EX4 9ER or telephone 0392 468556.